TREES

The Gardener's Collection

Better Homes and Gardens® Books

Des Moines

MEREDITH® BOOKS
President, Book Group: Joseph J. Ward
Vice President an Editorial Director: Elizabeth P. Rice
Art Director: Ernest Shelton

TREES
Senior Editor: Marsha Jahns
Editor: Debra D. Felton
Art Director: Michael Burns
Copy Editors: Durrae Johanek, Kay Sanders
Assistant Editor: Jennifer Weir
Administrative Assistant: Carla Horner
Special thanks to: Thomas Wirth

*All of us at Meredith® Books are dedicated to providing you
with the information and ideas you need to garden successfully. We guarantee your satisfaction with this book for as
long as you own it. If you have any questions, comments, or
suggestions,*
please write to us at:

MEREDITH® BOOKS, Garden Books
Editorial Department, RW 240
1716 Locust St.,
Des Moines, IA 50309-3023

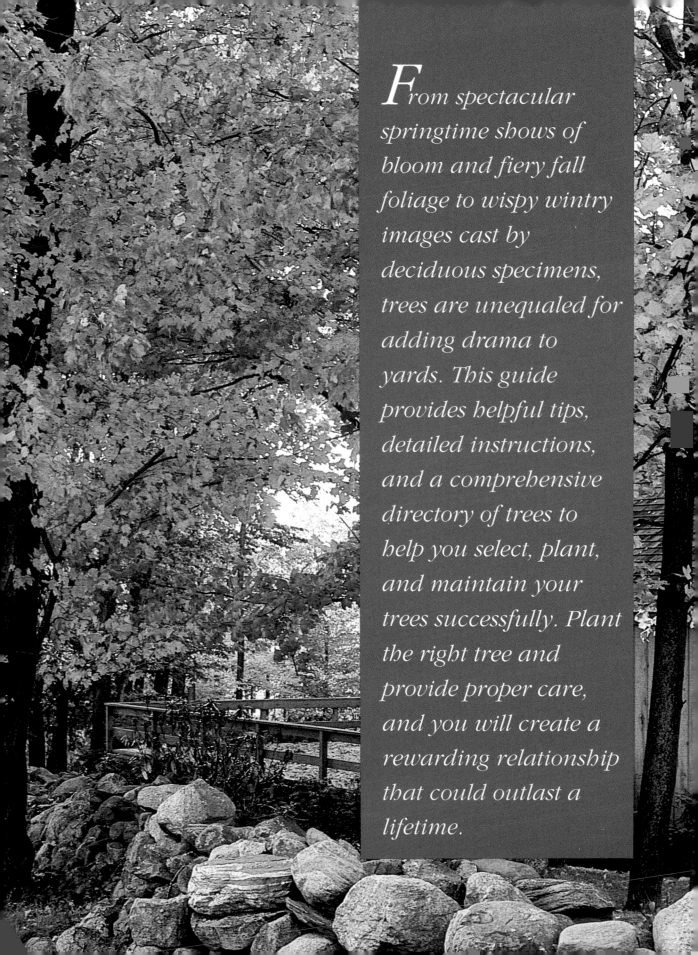

*F*rom spectacular springtime shows of bloom and fiery fall foliage to wispy wintry images cast by deciduous specimens, trees are unequaled for adding drama to yards. This guide provides helpful tips, detailed instructions, and a comprehensive directory of trees to help you select, plant, and maintain your trees successfully. Plant the right tree and provide proper care, and you will create a rewarding relationship that could outlast a lifetime.

CONTENTS

SELECTING A TREE TO FIT YOUR NEEDS 6

Choosing the Right Tree................8

Tree Types and Shapes................10

Placing Trees...................11

Flowering Trees..........................12

Autumn Colors 14

Choosing Trees for
Special Needs 16

Trees by Shape............................18

PLANTING AND MAINTAINING TREES 20

Planting a Tree 22

Training a Young Tree 26

Feeding Trees 27

Pruning and Repairs.....................28

When Pruning Is Needed 30

Cutting Off a Large Limb 34

Repairing Damage on
Older Trees..................................36

Preparing Trees for
Winter's Rigors............................38

Moving Trees 39

DIRECTORY OF TREES 40

ZONE MAP   62

INDEX   64

Selecting a Tree to Fit Your Needs

Trees, like people, have different needs, and some will thrive in areas where others won't. On the pages that follow, you'll find all the information you need to choose a tree that's a good fit for you and your landscape.

Choosing the Right Tree

Rate of growth is a number-one consideration. Some trees mature at a moderate rate. The green ash, for example, is a vigorous tree while young, eventually slowing its growth to develop a broad crown.

Fast-growing trees, on the other hand, will provide shade sooner, but may have certain drawbacks. They need a lot of water, sometimes plugging sewer lines as the roots reach out to any available source of moisture. The large roots also lift sidewalks if trees are planted too close to them. And the large limbs of some fast-growing shade trees can be broken easily by wind or ice.

The size of your house and lot are considerations, too. Lofty trees often blend with older homes on large lots, but low, ranch-style homes mix well with the horizontal branching of smaller trees.

Small shade trees, such as Russian olive or amur maple, work well on today's pocket-size properties. A Japanese maple can fit into a 9-foot-square area without impeding traffic—and it doesn't require constant pruning to keep it in bounds. Dogwood, redbud, and crab apple are also suitable.

The soil around your home helps to determine what will grow and what won't. 'Marshall's Seedless' ash (a green ash variety) and the Japanese pagoda tree flourish in dry soils that are hard to keep watered—those with slopes or open southern exposures. Weeping willow, larch, holly, red maple, and sweet gum can thrive in low, wet ground.

Temperatures limit your selections, too. Wind and cold are a ferocious duo, but some trees, such as white ash, white oak, Scotch pine, and Siberian elm, are hardy enough to survive both.

Coniferous evergreens can stand alone as specimens or serve as screens, windbreaks, or backdrops for flowering trees or shrubs. The dense foliage of broad-leaved evergreen trees makes the trees effective as specimen groups or as screens or borders.

Tree Types and Shapes

There are different types of shade trees, each offering various shading characteristics. The list below will help you find the perfect shade tree for your yard.

Pyramidal-shaped trees, such as pin oak, red horse chestnut, and small-leaved linden, are excellent for placement on average-size lawns or along streets. They must be spaced widely to permit light to penetrate beneath them so grass will not be shaded out. Avoid planting them directly in front of windows. Their dense foliage will hide the home and block the view.

Weeping shade trees, such as beech, willow, and European ash, need open spaces. They spread as wide as they are tall. Most city lots will accommodate only the smaller weeping trees.

Vase-shaped trees, such as red and white oak, sugar maple, and sycamore, grow tall, with top branches spreading somewhat wider than bottom ones. They make wonderful backyard trees where lots of shade is needed. Too many vase-shaped trees in a small area, however, make lawns difficult to maintain because of lack of sunlight.

Rounded trees, such as maple, hawthorn, and serviceberry, cause few problems for lawns. Their branching makes them suitable for planting along the street. They also make beautiful front lawn specimens.

Columnar trees, such as birch and poplar, are tall and slender. They're excellent when planted close together along property lines to screen views and provide a windbreak.

Gardener's Tip

In general, trees that reach a height of 20 feet or more should be planted at least 15 feet from any structure to keep their roots away from the foundation. Never plant such a tree near utility lines or under a roof overhang.

Placing Trees

Each tree variety has its own spacing and growth requirements. That's why it's wise to consult with the staff at a tree nursery before making a purchase. Then, before you start digging, select a spot where the tree will provide adequate shade where you need it. Locate trees to frame the house, choosing those that will stay in scale with the size of your home and its architectural features.

Small trees, such as dwarf-type fruit trees, are ideal for small lots because you can plant them close together without interfering with other gardening. Place trees about 10 feet apart (or far enough that their branches don't entwine when mature) and at least 8 feet from your house.

Spreading trees, such as oak, maple, linden, and elm, need at least 65 feet between their trunks. When they're too close together, there will be too much shade for grass to grow. Plant your large trees 30 feet from your house and 10 feet from walks, drives, and patios.

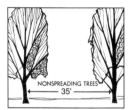

Nonspreading trees less than 35 feet high, such as hybrid maple, need 35 feet between trunks. Tall and narrow columnar trees (gray birch, white poplar, and Lombardy poplar are a few) can be planted even closer together.

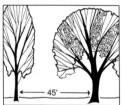

A nonspreading tree with a spreading tree can create problems because the larger tree will compete with the smaller one for sunlight and nutrients. Plant them at least 45 feet apart. If your yard doesn't permit this much space, plant shrubs instead.

Flowering Trees

The splashes of color from flowering trees can be a dazzling addition to your landscape. To make the most of their beauty, choose and place them carefully. For the greatest interest, select a tree that's different from your neighbors', perhaps one that blooms a little earlier or later with a different shade of yellow, purple, red, white, or pink.

Always consider the hues of surrounding plants, outdoor furniture, and buildings when choosing a flowering tree. Plant flowering trees in your lawn for viewing as sculptural elements. Or place them near enough to the house to enjoy at close range.

The shape of the tree will influence its position in your landscape. Some flowering trees have wide-spreading or weeping umbrella shapes; others form densely branched ovals or mounds. Columnar trees can work as accents or hedges. And some flowering trees grow large enough to act as shade trees, especially if pruned to encourage upward branching. Smaller types, branching close to the ground, make good screens or specimen clusters.

Full sun or shade? Many flowering trees, such as cherry, crab apple, and plum, thrive best in open spaces with full sun. The purple-leaved plum and other trees with colored foliage demand full sun for maximum color. Other species, including serviceberry, sorrel tree, and flowering dogwood, tolerate or even prefer light shade.

Blooms appear on most flowering trees in the spring, but some, like the Japanese pagoda tree, sorrel tree, and yellowwood, bloom in mid- to late summer. Many flowering trees also bear fruit that attracts wildlife. A number of them have interesting bark; consider the light gray bark of magnolia, the black trunk of redbud, or the cherrylike bark of tree lilac.

The purplish pink blooms of the redbud tree completely coat the tree's branches. An American native, the redbud may grow 25 feet tall, but it stays compact enough for small gardens.

Large masses of crab apple flowers extend from the tips of the branches almost to the center of the tree. Columnar varieties take little space, so they can be planted along property lines. Others are low and spreading or weeping. These forms are natural and need little pruning.

Autumn Colors

Shorter days and cooler nights bring on the annual tree extravaganza of fall colors. Use these colors to add dazzle to your landscape.

Many large trees sparkle in autumn. Beech, birch, sour gum, sweet gum, sugar and red maples, ash, and oak are just a sampling. Among smaller trees, autumn standouts are pear, sorrel tree, dogwood, and Japanese maple.

Plan the setting for these trees carefully. Provide autumn show-offs with a backdrop of evergreens, or create a counterpoint between their foliage and the color of your house, whether a pastel shade or a deep, dark tone.

For added drama, many trees offer more than one autumn asset. For example, beeches sport golden or bronze leaves and silvery bark. Birches have yellow leaves and textured white bark. Japanese maples combine fiery red or orange-yellow foliage with elegant, delicate texture and form. Many crab apples, after dropping their leaves, are covered with a spectacular fruit display.

As summer ends, the colors that dance in a bonfire take over deciduous trees. Yellows, reds, and oranges mingle. The results are breathtaking with rich bronzes and deep russets. Foliage and fruit hues vary from year to year depending on the weather.

You can count on showy reds every fall, but they turn even more vivid when the days are sunny and

Gardener's Tip

Intense afternoon sun strengthens color, so the western sides of trees often carry the most brilliant hues in early autumn—something to remember when deciding where to put new deciduous trees.

The fan-shaped leaves of ginkgo turn a sunny yellow, then fall off all at once, making raking a one-time effort.

the nights are cooler than 45 degrees. Trees in hollows will be the first to color because the cold air settles to low spots and works its magic on chemicals in the leaves.

The most vibrant colors appear after a warm, dry summer and early autumn rains. But a long rainy season in late fall makes them drab.

There's a subtle sequence in the show of fall color, although most of it happens in September and October. Trees and shrubs usually average two weeks of bright color.

Most of the berries and other fruits prized for their fall color stay bright through the winter—or invite fine-feathered visitors to dine.

Choosing Trees for Special Needs

Trees for Dense Shade
Crab apple
Dogwood
Maple
Oak
Spruce
Tulip tree

Trees for Filtered Shade
Birch
Ginkgo
Pine

Spring Flowering Trees
Butternut
Cherry, Sargent
Crab apple
Dogwood
Fruit trees
Hawthorn
Magnolia
Mountain ash
Pear, Bradford
Redbud
Serviceberry

Summer Flowering Trees
Catalpa
Chestnut, Chinese
Crape myrtle
Dogwood, Japanese
Franklinia
Fringe tree
Golden-chain tree
Golden-rain tree
Jacaranda
Linden
Silk tree
Sorrel

Tulip tree
Yellowwood

Trees for Fall Color
Dogwood
Ginkgo
Maple, amur
Maple, Norway
Maple, red
Maple, sugar
Oak, scarlet
Redbud
Sourwood

Trees for Winter Interest
Alder
Birch
Crab apple
Crape myrtle
Dogwood
Ginkgo
Holly
Katsura tree
Magnolia
Poplar
Oak
Oak, amur
Tulip tree
Tupelo, black
Willow

Fruiting Trees
Chinese jujube
Crab apple
Loquat
Pecan
Persimmon
Prunus species
Serviceberry

Fast Growing, Temporary Trees
Acacia
Alder
Catalpa
Elm, Siberian
Empress tree
Eucalyptus
Locust, black
Poplar
Silk tree
Tallow, Chinese
Willow

Fragrant Trees
Acacia
Arborvitae
Bayberry
Locust, black
Cedar
Crab apple
Eucalyptus
Fringe tree
Fruit trees
Hemlock
Katsura tree
Linden, littleleaf
Locust, black
Magnolia
Maple, amur
Pine
Russian olive
Silk tree
Silver-bell
Sorrel
Viburnum
Yellowwood

Gardener's Tip
Find out the light requirements of each tree. Sun-loving plants can survive in a shady location, but shade dwellers are not as tolerant and may die if planted in an exposed area.

Trees by Shape

Weeping Trees
Apricot, weeping
Ash, weeping European
Beech, weeping
Birch: Slender European, Young's
Boree, weeping
Cedar, deodar
Cherry, weeping
Crab apple, pink weeper
Hemlock, pendula
Hornbeam, weeping European
Linden, pendent silver
Pines (several varieties)
Spruce: Brewer, Koster
    weeping, blue
Willow (several varieties)

Pyramid-Shaped Trees
Beech
Birch
Black gum
Cedar
Hemlock
Holly
Larch
Linden
Magnolia
Pine
Oak, pin
Sorrel
Spruce
Sweet gum

Trees with Horizontal Branches
Chestnut, Chinese
Dogwood
Fir
Hawthorn
Oak (notably white and live oak)
Redbud
Pine, red
Pine, Scotch
Silk tree
Spruce

Columnar Trees
Arborvitae
Cedar, pyramidal red
Ginkgo, sentry
Hornbeam: Columnaris, Fastigiata
Juniper, blue columnar
Maple, red: Bowhill, Scanlon
Maple, sentry
Poplar, Lombardy
Tulip tree: Fastigiatum

Gardener's Tip
Always consider the growth rate of a plant before you buy. Fast-growing species may grow too quickly and have to be replaced in just a few years. If you want your landscaping project to look more established, spend the extra money and buy a larger specimen of a slow-growing species that won't have to be replaced or pruned so frequently.

The weeping willow has a graceful shape, although it is considered a messy tree.

Special Considerations

City Trees
Ash, green
Chestnut, horse
Crab apple
Fir, white
Ginkgo
Golden-rain tree
Hackberry
Hawthorn, Washington
Honey locust
Magnolia, saucer
Maple, Norway
Oak, red
Poplar, white
Spruce, Colorado

Avoid Near Street, Drive, Pipes
Ash
Catalpa
Chestnut, horse
Elder, box
Hawthorn
Honey locust
Locust, black
Maple, red
Maple, silver
Mulberry
Poplar
Walnut, black
Willow

Messy and Easily Broken Trees
Catalpa
Common mulberry
Eastern cottonwood
Elder, box
Hybrid poplar
Maple, silver
Russian olive
Tree-of-heaven
Willow, weeping

Planting and Maintaining Trees

The reason for selecting a certain tree may be as grand as accenting a new home or as simple as providing a windbreak. But the planting procedure is pretty much the same— whatever the tree, wherever you decide to place it.

Planting a Tree

Trees can be bought balled-and-burlapped, container grown, or bare root.

Balled-and-burlapped means they have been dug with a ball of soil left around the roots, then wrapped in burlap. Balled-and-burlapped or container-grown trees usually get off to a faster start than bare-root trees because fewer roots are disturbed in transplanting. They usually are more expensive, however.

Healthy trees should have green leaves and even growth. Branches on dormant, bare-root stock should be pliable.

Avoid buying a tree that has been damaged during shipment or mistreated at the nursery. The telltale signs: wilted foliage, broken branches, and scarred bark.

Examine the roots, if possible. A healthy root system will fill the soil in a container and grow out of drainage holes. Balled-and-burlapped trees should be tightly packed. Reject bare-root trees that have dry or broken roots

When to plant. The time to plant depends, in part, on the site and the kind of tree you select. A slope facing south can be used earlier in the spring than one facing north. Shaded areas are slower to warm up, but this shade can reduce dehydration of roots and leaves during and after planting. And planting can start sooner where soils are loamy and well-drained, not heavy and damp.

Digging and planting in the fall—instead of spring—carry certain advantages. Rainfall is less and soil is often in better working condition. The warm soil and cool air stimulate root growth. However, the new tree then faces the long winter with a limited root system for support. Plant tender trees and most broad-leaved evergreens in the spring.

Trees can be planted any time of the year that the ground can be worked, but spring and fall are the ideal times to plant most types.

Planting a Tree

When adding a tree to your landscape, keep in mind that it will be a permanent fixture. Proper planting is essential for your long-term enjoyment.

Because most trees need sun, plant a new tree where it will not be shaded by buildings or larger trees. Consider the tree's mature size and shape, and don't locate it where it will eventually grow into other plants or your home.

Planting instructions are similar for bare-root, balled-and-burlapped, or containerized trees, but we've selected a balled-and-burlapped specimen to illustrate.

Step 1: Dig a hole. If you must delay planting, keep the tree in a cool, shaded area, and water until it can be set into the ground. Soak roots of bare-root trees in a bucket of water for 24 hours before planting. To plant a balled-and-burlapped tree, first dig a hole twice as wide and at least 1½ times as deep as the root ball of the tree. This prevents crowding or damaging the roots and allows room for growth.

Step 2: Position the tree. Although trees vary in their soil preferences, most do best in well-drained soils. To improve soil, spade in organic matter and a source of phosphorus, such as superphosphate. Place the improved soil in the bottom of the hole so that the top of the root ball will be even with ground level. Position the tree so its best side faces the direction you'll be viewing it from.

Step 3: Backfill the hole. Cut the cord around the root ball, being careful not to damage

the trunk or roots. Roll back the burlap wrap, but do not remove it. The burlap will help keep the soil intact so the root ball is not disturbed. In time, the burlap will disintegrate. Backfill the planting hole with improved soil until it is about half full. Tamp down the soil with your feet, holding the tree in a straight, upright position.

Step 5: Stake trunk for support. Newly planted trees should be staked to give them strength against high winds. For trees with trunks between 1 and 3 inches across, use two stakes; trunks over 3 inches thick need three evenly spaced stakes. Stakes should be tall enough to secure the tree just below the spot where the major branches split away from the trunk. Tie tree with heavy cord.

Step 4: Water deeply. Fill the planting hole with water and allow it to drain completely. This will eliminate any air pockets and ensure that roots will be in contact with soil particles. After the water has drained, fill the planting hole to the top with improved soil. Make a catch basin for water by creating a raised circle of soil 2 to 3 inches high about a foot from the tree.

Gardener's Tip

Reduce moisture loss around a newly planted tree by applying a layer of mulch 2 to 3 inches thick. Use semi-decayed wood chips, pine bark, well-decayed manure, peat moss, or leaf mold. Keep mulch away from the trunk to reduce damage caused by rodents and decay.

Training a Young Tree

1. Proper training ensures that young trees planted as whips mature into beautifully shaped trees. Immediately after planting, make a cut at about a 6-foot height, above a bud, to force branching.

2. After the second growing season, remove unwanted branches. This selective pruning leaves a strong, graceful foundation for later growth.

3. Growth in the third year forms the basis of the tree's ultimate shape. Well-spaced branches with strong crotches and a single leader will mature into a specimen tree.

Feeding a Tree

Large trees benefit from being fed every three to four years. Early spring or late fall are the best times. Use a complete fertilizer with a nutrient ratio such as 10-6-4 for trees that do not flower, and 5-10-5 for the ones that do. Feeding methods are described below.

Broadcasting Trees in a lawn can be surface-fed by applying fertilizer at a distance of 2½ feet from the trunk to 2 to 3 feet beyond the spread of the tree's branches. Use fertilizer at a rate of 1 pound per inch of trunk diameter for trees 3 inches across or less, and 3 pounds per inch of trunk diameter for trees over 3 inches across.

The crowbar method For the crowbar method, make holes in the ground for fertilizer with a crowbar or auger at the rate of 10 to 15 per inch of trunk diameter. Holes should be made at least 2 feet from the base of the trunk. Feeder roots of younger trees are just inside the drip line (at the farthest tip of branches), and those of mature trees are outside the drip line. Space holes evenly around the perimeter. Feed at the rate of 2 to 3 pounds of fertilizer per inch of trunk diameter if the tree's diameter is less than 6 inches and 3 to 4 pounds of fertilizer per inch of trunk diameter if it's more than 6 inches. Mix fertilizer with the soil and pour it into the holes; do not use more than 1 cup of fertilizer per hole. Water well.

The root feeder method To inject fertilizer directly into the root zone, use a commercial root feeder. Fill the chamber with a compressed plant-food cartridge, attach a garden hose to the feeder, and turn on the water. These feeders can also be used for deep-watering roots during periods of drought.

Pruning and Repairs

There are many reasons for pruning a tree, depending on the tree's health and your preference. You might want to prune:

■ to remove diseased, dead, or broken branches;

■ to shape for special purposes—as a shaped specimen or to screen an eyesore, for example;

■ to renew old plants;

■ to eliminate suckers and wild growth;

■ to hold a tree within bounds;

■ to produce new fall growth for winter color;

■ to ensure production of larger flowers or fruits; or

■ to aid in transplanting—by compensating root loss.

But where to prune and how much? Here are a few guidelines.

Timing Early spring or late winter—when deciduous trees are free of foliage—is a good time to prune trees. At these times, you can see the arrangement of branches and can expect faster healing of large cuts.

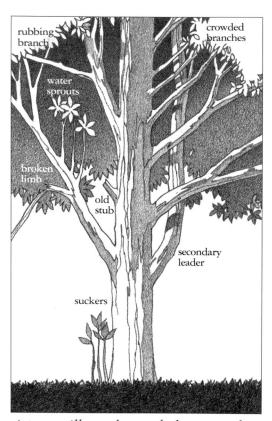

A tree will need your help a number of times during its life. Shown here are some situations that may cause problems if unremedied. Rubbing branches, broken limbs, and old stubs can allow insects to enter. Water sprouts and suckers tax a tree's strength. Narrow crotches and crowded branches create weak growth and are unsightly.

Transplants Branches and twigs of transplanted trees (except evergreens) must be pruned by about one-third to balance the loss of roots when the tree was dug. Leaves lose moisture as quickly as roots can take it in. If roots are cut without the branches being pruned proportionately, the plant may die of dehydration.

First pruning It should be done at planting time to aid in tree growth (see page 22). Prune branches that might be on a collision course with a building or power line. If branches are cut when small, wounds will heal faster.

Flowering trees These small trees, such as crab apple and dogwood, are pruned much like other trees, although two or three "leaders" should be left untouched. Most flowering trees should be pruned at the end of blossom time.

A few principles Heavy pruning on top causes leaves and branches to grow. Heavy pruning of the

Gardener's Tip

Has there been any excavating near your trees, or has the grade level around them been changed? Nearby construction in the past 15 years can result in tree root damage long after the building is completed.

roots lessens vegetative growth (leaves) but increases production of flowers and fruit. Heading-back—or cutting back tips—of new growth forces development of lateral branching.

If two branches rub, remove the smaller of the two. A tree should have only one main trunk. A secondary leader is no problem when the tree is small. However, after branches grow larger and heavier, the V-shaped crotch weakens and the tree may split in high winds or snowstorms. Even a small split offers easy entry for insects.

When Pruning Is Needed

On the following four pages, you'll find the common situations that call for pruning, and the tools to use in each instance.

The tools of the trimming trade range from three basic ones to a shed full of specialized implements Home gardeners find pruning shears handy for light pruning and trimming. A saw is needed for larger branches. Hand loppers—long-handled and requiring the use of both hands—let you prune higher sprouts and thicker twigs.

Gardener's Tip

Pruning large tree limbs and high branches is best left to a professional tree service or arborist. Also, fill small hollows and squirrel holes yourself, but filling larger ones, especially those marked with fungi, will require the help of a specialist.

Crossed branches or those rubbing against each other create wounds that are constantly open to insects and disease. Using pruning shears, remove one offender and trim the wound of the other.

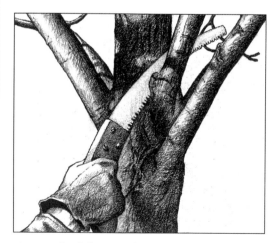

Crowded branches never develop to full size. Large branches compete with small, and the small ones become targets for disease and breakage. Use a pruning saw to remove limbs that contribute least to the shape of the tree.

Although they're small, they tax the strength of the tree. Cut off water sprouts, using pruning shears or long-handled loppers.

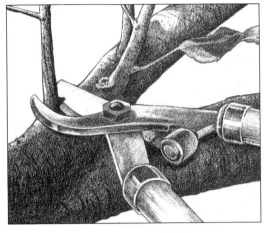

Water sprouts are soft, fast-growing branches usually shooting out from the trunk or large limbs.

Closely spaced limbs, or one growing just above the other from a major limb, create a source of weak growth. Remove the smaller of the two or the one that is less needed for the shape of the tree.

Low branches shade out grass and hamper lawn mowing. If a tree has several low branches, remove only one or two each season. On mature shade trees, the lowest branch should be at least 6 feet above the ground.

Broken or injured branches are removed by making a cut as close to the parent limb as possible. Repair soon after damage occurs. Such breaks can peel bark back to the main branch, offering easy entry to insects and disease.

Gardener's Tip

Remember, the position of branches does not change as the tree matures—a branch that is now a few feet off the ground will always be at about the same height. It won't rise much higher. Low branches on mature trees shade the grass and make mowing difficult.

Suckers are growths coming from the base of the trunk or from roots. Dig down to where they attach and make a cut flush with the trunk or root. If any of the sucker remains, pruning only induces more shoots.

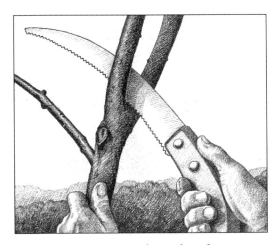

Double or secondary leaders sometimes develop on young trees. They're not a problem when trees are small, but after branches are heavy the crotch becomes weak and may split in high winds.

Girdling roots are large ones that wrap around the base of the tree. They're not only unsightly, they also gradually cut off the flow of nutrients. Cut off roots at their origin and remove all that touch the trunk.

How to Cut Off a Large Limb

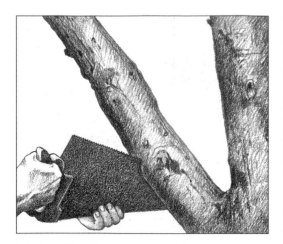

Make the first cut on the underside of the limb, about 15 inches from the trunk. This will keep the bark from tearing when you make the final cut. Cut about one-fourth of the way through, or until the saw "pinches."

Make the second cut on the top side of the limb, about 4 inches beyond the first cut. Saw all the way through. When the branch falls, the bark will strip back to the cut on the underside of the stub.

Gardener's Tip

Applying normal paint, shellac, or asphalt to tree wounds can cause problems. The coating eventually cracks and allows moisture to accumulate underneath, creating an ideal environment for rot. Instead, use products made specifically for dressing tree wounds.

Remove the stub or it may cause decay. Support the stub as you cut, or its weight will strip bark from the trunk. Make sure the cut is flush so bark can grow around it.

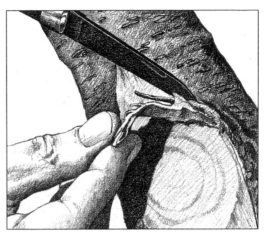

Trim the bark around all wounds until the edges are solidly attached to the wood. The final trim should be oval. Wounds shaped in this way heal much faster than round ones.

Heavy branches on trees can be dangerous for amateur tree-trimmers. Tie a heavy rope around the branch and attach it securely to the trunk or a sturdy higher limb before you saw. If the job requires climbing, leave it to a professional.

Gardener's Tip

When you're pruning crossed, crowded, or damaged branches of a tree, it's best to cut just beyond the branch collar, usually a series of ridges, instead of absolutely flush. Flush cutting delays healing and tends to cause uneven formation of a callus, thus encouraging the onset of decay.

Repairing Injuries

If a branch dies, remove the dead wood, making sure to cut *outside* the callus. Opening the callus exposes the tree to pest infestation.

When bark has been damaged, you may be able to promote healing if the bark is still intact—or cleanly broken off—and still moist. Nail the bark back in place, spread wet paper towels over the wound, then wrap the dressing securely in white plastic for about three weeks

If that kind of first aid is unfeasible, wait one growing season to see how much bark loosens around the wound. Then carefully trim away the loose bark with a knife or chisel. Make the cut as smooth an oval or circle as possible; avoid cutting a sharp V at the top or bottom.

To reinforce a structurally weak tree, especially if a break would endanger people or property, call in professionals to stretch steel rods or cables between large branches.

To prevent injuries to beautiful trees such as the winged euonymus above and the horse chestnut opposite, proper care is a must. The euonymus is actually a shrub that was pruned into tree form.

Prepare Trees for Winter's Rigors

Along with unpacking winter coats and checking the antifreeze, wise home gardeners also prepare their trees for winter. Apply mulches, 3 to 6 inches deep, to broad-leaved shrubs and newly planted trees when the ground freezes.

Cold, drying winds are especially damaging to broad-leaved evergreens and also can be a hazard to needled evergreens, such as pine and juniper. Antidesiccant sprays can help reduce the drying. They form a film on leaf surfaces. Spray once in November and again in January or February.

Soak evergreens thoroughly in February. Those on the south and west sides of the house are the first to suffer because they are exposed to the sun longer and the frost comes out of the ground faster on those sides. Turn the garden hose on slowly so only ½ inch of water spouts up when you hold the hose upright. Or use a water lance to put water to the root zone. Let the water run near the evergreen's base for four hours or up to all day—until the soil can't absorb any more water.

To prevent snow damage to evergreens and young trees, bind branches of small trees close together to prevent accumulation. Knock snow off larger ones.

An ice storm calls for a quick survey of damage. Quick-growing trees (such as poplars, willows, elms, and maples) and older ones are susceptible. Trim broken branches so they're flush with the main branch or trunk. If the weather is above freezing, treat the wound with shellac or tree asphalt paint.

Gardener's Tip

If you're thinking of moving a tree, keep this in mind: Trees shorter than 6 feet and with trunks less than 1 inch can be moved by you. Larger trees should be transplanted by professionals.

Moving Trees

Sometimes the major snag in landscaping or remodeling is that beautiful trees are in the way. Rather than ax your plans—or your plants—move smaller trees. Here's how.

Tackling your trees. Deciduous plants are best moved when dormant in spring or fall so roots can get established before supplying water to leaves. Evergreens can be moved in spring or late summer so they can take root before summer heat or winter cold. Summer is not a good time to shift plants, but by keeping roots protected and moist, you can reduce the risk.

Use a sharp spade to cut around the roots, cutting as few as possible. When the tree can be rocked, wrap the roots in burlap with as much soil intact as possible. To avoid damaging the tree, get help hauling the heavy root ball.

Keep the roots moist and allow minimal exposure. Dig a hole twice as wide and 1½ times as deep as

To prevent the topsoil from washing away, distribute water slowly and evenly with a canvas soaker hose.

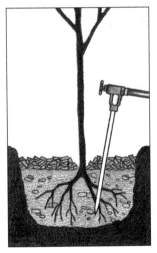

Use a water lance to deliver water straight to the roots with minimum waste. Mulch around the tree's base to further reduce water loss.

the root ball. Add improved soil, such as compost, until the top of the ball and the ground are level. Position the tree. Cut the cord and pull back the burlap (it will rot away). Fill the hole halfway, water, tamp the soil, and repeat until filled. Water often and stake the tree if needed.

DIRECTORY OF TREES

Carefully chosen trees are the backbone of a successful landscape. To make the most of your long-term investment, check the treasury of trees on the following pages. By choosing a tree based on the characteristics and growing conditions that meet your needs, you'll enjoy spectacular shade, color, and beauty for years to come.

Directory of Trees

ALDER
Alnus sp.

European
A. glutinosa

Type: Deciduous

Fall Foliage: Brown

Shade Density: Medium to light

Height/Width: 75 feet/40 feet

Zone: 4

Soil Preference: Tolerant; takes wet conditions

Comments: Flower catkins present in winter.

Italian
A. cordata

Type: Deciduous

Fall Foliage: Brown

Shade Density: Medium to light

Height/Width: 60 feet/25 feet

Zone: 6

Soil Preference: Tolerant; takes wet conditions

Comments: Flower catkins present in winter.

ARBORVITAE
Thuja sp.

Oriental
Platycladus orientalis

Type: Coniferous

Shade Density: Dense

Height: 50 feet; width varies with variety

Zone: 4

Soil Preference: Moist, well-drained soil

Comments: Use as specimen tree or hedge.

White Cedar
Thuja occidentalis

Type: Coniferous

Shade Density: Dense

Height/Width: 50 feet tall; width varies with variety

Zone: 2

Soil Preference: Moist, well-drained soil

Comments: Use as specimen tree, or shear and use in foundation plantings. Dense, scalelike foliage. Easily damaged in storms.

ASH
Fraxinus sp.

Green
F. pennsylvanica 'lanceolata'
Type: Deciduous
Fall Foliage: Yellow, purple
Shade Density: Light
Height/Width: 60 feet/25 feet
Zone: 2
Soil Preference: Tolerant
Comments: Little care. Use as specimen tree. 'Marshall's Seedless' is a popular variety.'

White
F. americana
Type: Deciduous
Fall Foliage: Yellow, purple
Shade Density: Light
Height/Width: 90 feet/45 feet
Zone: 4
Soil Preference: Tolerant
Comments: Volunteer seedlings can become a problem.

ASPEN, UPRIGHT EUROPEAN
Populus tremula 'erecta'
Type: Deciduous
Shade Density: Dense
Height/Width: 50 feet/10 feet
Zone: 2
Soil Preference: Tolerant
Comments: Tall columnar tree, perfect for narrow spaces or to create visual barrier. Resists canker that infects Lombardy poplar. Likes full sun; very hardy.

BALD CYPRESS
Taxodium distichum
Type: Deciduous
Fall Foliage: Reddish brown
Shade Density: Medium
Height/Width: 70 feet/30 feet
Zone: 5
Soil Preference: Well-drained, moist, acid
Comments: Deciduous conifer with soft texture and slender pyramidal shape. Distinctive in a grove or by water's edge; adapts to wet or dry soil.

Directory of Trees

BEECH
Fagus sp.

American
F. grandifolia

Type: Deciduous

Fall Foliage: Yellow, gold

Shade Density: Dense

Height/Width: 40 feet/60 feet

Zone: 4

Soil Preference: Tolerant, but prefers moist areas

Comments: Occasional inedible nuts. Lower branches drop off. Shallow root system; must not be disturbed.

European
F. sylvatica

Type: Deciduous

Fall Foliage: Yellow, gold

Shade Density: Dense

Height/Width: 90 feet/50 feet

Zone: 5

Soil Preference: Tolerant, but prefers acid soil

Comments: Occasional inedible nuts. Shallow root system; must not be disturbed.

BIRCH
Betula sp.

Canoe or Paper
B. papyrifera

Type: Deciduous

Fall Foliage: Yellow

Shade Density: Medium to light

Height/Width: 90 feet/40 feet

Zone: 2

Soil Preference: Tolerant, but prefers moist areas

Comments: Beautiful white bark peels naturally. Grows in clumps of two to four trunks.

River
B. nigra

Type: Deciduous

Fall Foliage: Yellow

Shade Density: Medium

Height/Width: 40 feet/30 feet

Zone: 5

Soil Preference: Moist, acid soil

Comments: Peeling bark with layers of gray and reddish brown. Resists birch borer; tolerates wet soil. Often develops multiple trunks; use in naturalistic setting.

BOX ELDER
Acer negundo

Type: Deciduous

Fall Foliage: Yellow, brown

Shade Density: Medium

Height/Width: 60 feet/30 feet

Zone: 2

Soil Preference: Very tolerant

Comments: Drought-, heat-, and cold-resistant. Can become pestiferous. Branches break easily.

BUCKEYE, OHIO
Aesculus glabra

Type: Deciduous

Fall Foliage: Brilliant orange

Shade Density: Medium

Height/Width: 30 feet/30 feet

Zone: 4

Soil Preference: Moist, well-drained soil

Comments: Use as specimen tree; 5- to 7-inch greenish white spike flowers in spring. Round 1- to 2-inch shiny brown inedible nuts in fall. Soot-tolerant.

CATALPA
Catalpa speciosa

Type: Deciduous

Fall Foliage: Brown

Shade Density: Medium to dense

Height/Width: 60 feet/35 feet

Zone: 5

Soil Preference: Tolerant

Comments: Disease-resistant. Plant for shade. Handsome panicles of white flowers in midsummer, followed by curved cigar- or pencil-like seedpods. Often messy.

CEDAR
Cedrus sp.

Atlas or atlantic
C. atlantica

Type: Coniferous

Shade Density: Medium to dense

Height/Width: 60 feet/35 feet

Zone: 6

Soil Preference: Rich, well-drained soil

Comments: Produces 2x3-inch cones. Stiff branches often droop slightly. Use as specimen tree. Doesn't do well in close plantings.

CRAB APPLE
Malus sp.

Type: Deciduous

Fall Foliage: Yellow, orange, brown

Shade Density: Light to medium

Height/Width: 10–50 feet/20 feet Average: 15 feet/15 feet

Zone: Varies

Soil Preference: Rich, well-drained soil

Comments: Grows in almost any climate in U.S. Produces single, double, or semidouble, 1- to 2-inch white or pink flowers in spring followed by ½-inch yellow, green, or red fruits; good in jellies and for birds. Use as specimen tree or in rows along drive.

DOGWOOD
Cornus sp.

Flowering
C. florida

Type: Deciduous

Fall Foliage: Orange, brown, red

Shade Density: Light

Height: 15–30 feet

Zone: 5

Soil Preference: Well-drained soil

Comments: Use as specimen tree or accent plant. Best in lightly shaded areas. Has 3- to 5-inch, pink or white single flowers. Most varieties bear red inedible berries.

Japanese
C. kousa

Type: Deciduous

Fall Foliage: Orange, red, brown

Shade Density: Light

Height: 20 feet

Zone: 6

Soil Preference: Well-drained soil

Comments: Bears 3- to 5-inch white flowers, occasionally tinged with pink. Three-quarter-inch red inedible fruits relished by birds are produced in late summer. Use as specimen.

ELM
Ulmus sp.

American
U. americana

Type: Deciduous

Fall Foliage: Yellow, brown

Shade Density: Medium

Height/Width: 110 feet/40 feet

Zone: 2

Soil Preference: Tolerant

Comments: Large, long-lived tree; slightly pendulous branches. Beautiful as specimen tree. Susceptible to Dutch elm disease.

Chinese
U. parvifolia

Type: Deciduous; evergreen in warm areas

Fall Foliage: Red, yellow, brown

Shade Density: Medium

Height/Width: 50 feet/40 feet

Zone: 5

Soil Preference: Tolerant

Comments: Fast growing, with attractive gray peeling bark on mature trees. Use as specimen tree or screen. Self-sows and can become a problem.

Siberian
U. pumila

Type: Deciduous

Fall Foliage: Yellow, brown

Shade Density: Medium to dense

Height/Width: 65 feet/50 feet

Zone: 4

Soil Preference: Tolerant

Comments: Fast growing. Use in screen. Resistant to Dutch elm disease. Easily damaged in storms.

Smoothleaf
U. carpinifolia

Type: Deciduous

Fall Foliage: Yellow, brown

Shade Density: Medium to dense

Height/Width: 80 feet/70 feet (other varieties smaller)

Zone: 5

Soil Preference: Tolerant

Comments: Several varieties. Most fast growing, disease-resistant. Uniform growth. Use as lawn specimen, street tree, and accent for foundation plantings.

FIR, DOUGLAS
Pseudotsuga menziesi

Type: Coniferous

Shade Density: Dense

Height: 100 feet

Zone: 5

Soil Preference: Moist, well-drained soil

Comments: Hardy. Fast growing for a conifer. Can be sheared and used as a hedge or left to grow as impressive lawn specimen. Use in windbreaks and backgrounds. One-inch, bluish green, soft needles. Attractive.

FIR, WHITE
Abies concolor

Type: Coniferous

Shade Density: Dense

Height: 75 feet

Zone: 4

Soil Preference: Moist, well-drained soil

Comments: Hardy. Fast growing for a conifer. Use as specimen tree. Often loses lower branches as it matures. Fragrant 2-inch, blue-green needles.

GINKGO
(Maidenhair tree)
Ginkgo biloba

Type: Deciduous

Fall Foliage: Yellow

Shade Density: Medium to dense

Height/Width: 90 feet/40 feet

Zone: 5

Soil Preference: Tolerant

Comments: Slow growing. Insect and disease-free. Resistant to smog. All leaves fall off at same time in fall. Use as specimen tree only where space permits. Buy nonfruiting forms because fruit produces obnoxious odor.

Golden-chain tree *A dazzling late-May floral display is your colorful compensation for planting a golden-chain tree. Lasting as long as two weeks, the pendulous, 16-inch-long flower clusters hang like jewels from every branch. This tree begins blooming the first season after you plant it. Within several years, the tree will reach a mature height of 30 feet.*

GUM, SWEET
Liquidambar styraciflua

Type: Deciduous

Fall Foliage: Yellow, red, gold

Shade Density: Medium to dense

Height/Width: 70 feet/50 feet

Zone: 6

Soil Preference: Tolerant, but best in moist, well-drained soil

Comments: Fast growing in moist areas. Disease-resistant and pest-free. Bark is attractive silver gray. Prickly, round seed clusters form on mature trees in fall and cling through part of winter. Plant in wet areas.

HACKBERRY
Celtis occidentalis

Type: Deciduous

Fall Foliage: Yellow, brown

Shade Density: Medium to dense

Height/Width: 75 feet/50 feet

Zone: 4

Soil Preference: Tolerant, but best in moist, well-drained soil

Comments: Good for city planting. Soot-resistant. One-half-inch berries are produced in fall. Warty bark.

Common varieties are susceptible to fungus disease called witches' broom.

HAWTHORN
Crataegus sp.

Downy
C. mollis

Type: Deciduous

Fall Foliage: Red, gold

Shade Density: Light to medium

Height/Width: 25 feet/15 feet

Zone: 5

Soil Preference: Tolerant

Comments: Stiff 1-inch thorns. Covered with white flowers in early spring. Pear-shaped red fruit in fall.

Paul's scarlet
C. laevigata 'pauli'

Type: Deciduous

Shade Density: Light to medium

Height/Width: 25 feet/10 feet

Zone: 5

Soil Preference: Tolerant

Comments: Double white flowers in spring. Scarlet fruit in fall.

Single seed
C. monogyna

Type: Deciduous

Fall Foliage: Red, gold

Shade Density: Medium to light

Height/Width: 30 feet/20 feet

Zone: 5

Soil Preference: Tolerant

Comments: Stiff 1-inch thorns; small white flowers followed by ⅜-inch red fruits in fall. Slightly pendulous branches.

HEMLOCK
Tsuga canadensis

Type: Coniferous

Shade Density: Dense

Height: 50 feet

Zone: 2

Soil Preference: Moist; slightly acid soil

Comments: Use as specimen tree or shear for hedge and screen. Flat ½-inch, dark green needles. Slightly pendulous branches.

HICKORY
Shagbark
Carya ovata

Type: Deciduous

Fall Foliage: Gold, brown

Shade Density: Light to medium

Height/Width: 90 feet/50 feet

Zone: 5

Soil Preference: Tolerant

Comments: Use as background or specimen tree in large yard. Slate gray, loosely flaking bark. Tasty, edible nuts on mature trees in fall.

HONEY LOCUST, THORNLESS
Gleditsia triacanthos

Type: Deciduous

Fall Foliage: Yellow

Shade Density: Light to medium

Height: 40–70 feet (varies with variety)

Zone: 5

Soil Preference: Tolerant

Comments: Use in difficult city conditions where hardy tree is needed. Hybrids do not have thorns or seedpods like common honey locust. Foliage is fernlike and delicate. Plant in lawn and other areas where light shade is desired.

HORSE CHESTNUT
Aesculus sp.

Common
A. hippocastanum

Type: Deciduous

Fall Foliage: Yellow, brown

Shade Density: Medium to dense

Height/Width: 75 feet/40 feet

Zone: 3

Soil Preference: Moist, well-drained soil

Comments: Twelve- to 15-inch spikes of white flowers in spring, followed by 2- to 3-inch, inedible nuts. Massive when mature. Often messy. Soot-tolerant.

Red
A. x carnea

Type: Deciduous

Fall Foliage: Yellow, brown

Shade Density: Medium to dense

Height/Width: 40 feet/35 feet

Zone: 4

Soil Preference: Moist, well-drained soil

Comments: Five- to 8-inch spikes of red flowers in spring. Soot-tolerant. More hardy and less messy than common horse chestnut.

JUNIPER
Juniperus sp.

Chinese
J. chinensis

Type: Coniferous

Shade Density: Dense

Height: 50 feet

Zone: 4

Soil Preference: Well-drained soil

Comments: Use as specimen tree. Other varieties come in shrub and ground cover forms. Scalelike, pointed leaves.

Eastern red cedar
J. virginiana

Type: Coniferous

Shade Density: Dense

Height: 80 feet

Zone: 3

Soil Preference: Well-drained soil

Comments: Slow growing. Use as specimen or in windbreaks. One-half-inch blue berries are relished by birds. Scalelike, pointed leaves. Easily sheared.

LARCH, EUROPEAN
Larix decidua

Type: Deciduous

Fall Foliage: Yellow

Shade Density: Medium

Height: 60 feet

Zone: 2

Soil Preference: Moist; slightly acid soil

Comments: Needlelike foliage. Cones stay on year-round. Use as specimen. Branches slightly pendulous.

LINDEN
Tilia sp.

American
T. americana

Type: Deciduous

Fall Foliage: Yellow

Shade Density: Medium

Height/Width: 70 feet/40 feet

Zone: 2

Soil Preference: Moist, well-drained soil

Comments: Tiny white panicles in midsummer. Blue berries in late summer and fall. Not soot tolerant. Use as specimen tree.

Small-leaved European
T. cordata

Type: Deciduous

Fall Foliage: Yellow

Shade Density: Medium to dense

Height/Width: 70 feet/30 feet

Zone: 4

Soil Preference: Moist, well-drained soil

Comments: Fast, hardy growth. Soot-tolerant. Tiny, fragrant white panicles in midsummer. Blue berries in late summer and fall. Use as specimen tree.

MAGNOLIA
Magnolia sp.

Cucumber tree
M. acuminata

Type: Deciduous

Fall Foliage: Brown

Saucer magnolia *Spectacular white to purple flowers are the hallmark of this tree. In early May, the 5-inch, cup-shape blossoms open before the leaves appear. This ornamental tree, which grows 25 feet, starts blooming at a young age and is a good choice for small yards.*

Shade Density: Dense

Height/Width: 85 feet/30 feet

Zone: 5

Soil Preference: Rich, well-drained soil

Comments: Grow for shade. Inconspicuous flowers and colorful cucumber-shape seedpods. Branches often skirt ground. Beautiful, fast-growing specimen.

Saucer
M. x soulangiana

Type: Deciduous

Fall Foliage: Brown

Shade Density: Light

Height/Width: 25 feet/25 feet

Zone: 6

Soil Preference: Moist, well-drained soil

Comments: Use as specimen. Five- to 10-inch white-purple cup-shape flowers cover tree in early spring before leaves appear. Attractive slate gray bark.

MAPLE
Acer sp.

Amur
A. ginnala

Type: Deciduous

Fall Foliage: Scarlet

Shade Density: Medium to dense

Height/Width: 20 feet/20 feet

Zone: 2

Soil Preference: Tolerant

Comments: Can stand cold, heavy winds. Attractive in fall. Winged seeds relished by birds. Use as specimen tree or in hedges and screens.

Directory of Trees

Japanese
A. palmatum

Type: Deciduous

Fall Foliage: Scarlet

Shade Density: Medium to light

Height/Width: 20 feet/20 feet (other varieties smaller)

Zone: 6

Soil Preference: Moist, well-drained soil

Comments: Use as specimen or lawn tree. Red or red-green. Foliage finely cut. Often does best if planted in partial shade.

Norway
A. platanoides

Type: Deciduous

Fall Foliage: Bright yellow

Shade Density: Dense

Height/Width: 90 feet/50 feet

Zone: 4

Soil Preference: Tolerant

Comments: Fast growing. Hardy. Provides deep shade. Shallow root system makes plant growth beneath it almost impossible. Soot-tolerant. 'Crimson King' variety has red leaves.

Red
A. rubrum

Type: Deciduous

Fall Foliage: Red, orange

Shade Density: Medium

Height/Width: 70 feet/50 feet

Zone: 4

Soil Preference: Tolerant, if kept moist

Comments: Fast growing. Attractive red flowers and seeds. Deep green foliage. Occasionally suffers storm damage.

Silver
A. saccharinum

Type: Deciduous

Fall Foliage: Yellow, orange

Shade Density: Medium

Height/Width: 100 feet/80 feet

Zone: 3

Soil Preference: Tolerant, if kept moist

Comments: Fast growing. Finely cut leaves; silver undersides. Branches skirt ground. Roots can damage pavement. Occasionally suffers storm damage.

Sugar
A. saccharum

Type: Deciduous

Fall Foliage: Yellow, orange, red

Shade Density: Medium to dense

Height/Width: 75 feet/50 feet

Zone: 3

Soil Preference: Moist, well-drained soil

Comments: Grows more slowly than other maples. Not soot-tolerant. Source of maple syrup. Storm-sturdy.

MOUNTAIN ASH
Sorbus sp.

European
S. aucuparia

Type: Deciduous

Fall Foliage: Red, brown

Shade Density: Light to medium

Height/Width: 40 feet/30 feet

Zone: 3

Soil Preference: Well-drained soil

Comments: Use as lawn or specimen tree. Covered with 3- to 5-inch clusters of small white flowers in spring. One-fourth-inch red berries in fall. Treat for borers.

Korean
S. alnif4olia

Type: Deciduous

Fall Foliage: Orange, scarlet

Shade Density: Light to medium

Height/Width: 50 feet/30 feet

Zone: 5

Soil Preference: Well-drained soil

Comments: Use as lawn or street tree. Three-fourth-inch white blossoms followed by ½-inch red berries relished by birds in fall. Green, fernlike foliage. Low branches often skirt ground.

OAK
Quercus sp.

Pin
Q. palustris

Type: Deciduous

Fall Foliage: Scarlet

Shade Density: Medium

Height/Width: 75 feet/40 feet

Zone: 5

Soil Preference: Well-drained; slightly acid soil

Comments: Use as specimen tree. Hardy and storm-sturdy.

Directory of Trees

Red
Q. rubra

Type: Deciduous

Fall Foliage: Red

Shade Density: Medium

Height/Width: 75 feet/50 feet

Zone: 5

Soil Preference: Well-drained; slightly acid soil

Comments: Fastest-growing oak. Ornamental. Leaves cling to tree well into winter. Soot-resistant.

Scarlet
Q. coccinea

Type: Deciduous

Fall Foliage: Scarlet

Shade Density: Medium

Height/Width: 75 feet/60 feet

Zone: 4

Soil Preference: Well-drained; slightly acid soil

Comments: Fast growing. Use as shade or specimen tree. Does not transplant well.

Oak trees *Many types of oak trees provide brilliant fall color, while others are evergreen. They are excellent shade trees and grow from 50 feet tall to much higher.*

Shingle
Q. imbricaria

Type: Deciduous

Fall Foliage: Yellow, red

Shade Density: Medium

Height/Width: 75 feet/60 feet

Zone: 5

Soil Preference: Well-drained; slightly acid soil

Comments: Use as hedge or windbreak. Easily sheared. Leaves cling to tree into winter.

White
Q. alba

Type: Deciduous

Fall Foliage: Violet, purplish red

Shade Density: Medium to dense

Height/Width: 90 feet/80 feet

Zone: 4

Soil Preference: Well-drained; slightly acid soil

Comments: Slow growing; majestic when mature. Difficult to transplant.

Willow
Q. phellos

Type: Deciduous

Fall Foliage: Yellow

Shade Density: Medium

Height/Width: 60 feet/40 feet

Zone: 6

Soil Preference: Well-drained; slightly acid soil

Comments: Fast growing; shallow roots make transplanting easy. Use as specimen tree.

PEAR, 'BRADFORD' CALLERY
Pyrus calleryana 'bradford'

Type: Deciduous

Fall Foliage: Reddish purple

Shade Density: Dense

Height/Width: 35 feet/20 feet

Zone: 5

Soil Preference: Tolerant

Comments: Blight- and pest-resistant, symmetrical, and adaptable. Upright branches covered with white blooms in spring; no pears, however.

PINE
Pinus sp.

Austrian
P. nigra

Type: Coniferous

Shade Density: Dense

Height: 75 feet

Zone: 4

Soil Preference: Well-drained soil

Comments: Five-inch dark green needles in bundles of two. Use as specimen tree or in windbreak. Soot-resistant. Cones are 2 to 3 inches long.

Directory of Trees

Ponderosa
P. ponderosa

Type: Coniferous

Shade Density: Medium to dense

Height: 100 feet

Zone: 6

Soil Preference: Well-drained soil

Comments: Four- to 6-inch dark green needles in bundles of three. Fast growing. Large; ideal for specimen planting in large yards. Attractive brown platelike bark. Smaller variety is available.

Red
P. resinosa

Type: Coniferous

Shade Density: Dense

Height: 75 feet

Zone: 3

Soil Preference: Well-drained soil

Comments: Use as specimen tree or in windbreak. Four- to 6-inch dark green, flexible needles in bundles of two. Subject to pine bud moth infestation in some areas.

Scotch
P. sylvestris

Type: Coniferous

Shade Density: Dense

Height: 75 feet

Zone: 3

Soil Preference: Well-drained soil

Comments: Fast growing. Three-inch, blue-green needles in clumps. Red bark on mature trees. Hardy in seashore or city conditions. Drought-resistant.

Purple-leaved plum *From April through fall, this tree is a lovely show. Direct sun is needed for deep leaf color. Prune it to a single trunk while it's young, or it will have a shrub shape.*

White
P. strobus

Type: Coniferous

Shade Density: Medium to dense

Height: 100 feet

Zone: 3

Soil Preference: Well-drained soil

Comments: Two- to 5-inch light green needles in bundles of five. Mature specimens stately. Easily sheared and shaped.

POPLAR
Populas sp.

Lombardy
P. nigra 'italica'

Type: Deciduous

Fall Foliage: Yellow

Shade Density: Light

Height/Width: 90 feet/15 feet

Zone: 3

Soil Preference: Well-drained soil

Comments: Very fast growing. Useful for quick screens and windbreaks while other trees reach maturity. Short-lived and susceptible to canker disease.

White
P. alba

Type: Deciduous

Fall Foliage: Red, brown

Shade Density: Light to medium

Height/Width: 60 feet/50 feet

Zone: 3

Soil Preference: Well-drained soil

Comments: Fast growing. Use as specimen. Leaves have gray, fuzzy undersides. Canker-resistant columnar variety that lives longer is available.

REDBUD
(Judas tree)
Cercis canadensis

Type: Deciduous

Fall Foliage: Yellow

Shade Density: Light to medium

Height/Width: 35 feet/30 feet

Zone: 5

Soil Preference: Moist, well-drained soil

Comments: One-half-inch purple-pink blossoms cover tree in early spring. White and pure pink varieties available. Mix with other flowering trees for dramatic effect.

Directory of Trees

RUSSIAN OLIVE
Elaeagnus angustifolia

Type: Deciduous

Fall Foliage: Yellow, brown

Shade Density: Medium

Height/Width: 20 feet/20 feet

Zone: 2

Soil Preference: Tolerant

Comments: Attractive, silver-gray foliage with yellow-green berries in spring. Hardy, pest-resistant, and soot-tolerant. Peeling brown bark on mature specimens. Trunk often gnarled.

SPRUCE
Picea sp.

Colorado
P. pungens

Type: Coniferous

Shade Density: Dense

Height: 100 feet

Zone: 3

Soil Preference: Well-drained soil

Comments: Dark green to pale blue foliage. Use as specimen tree. Mature trees lose lower branches.

White
P. glauca

Type: Coniferous

Shade Density: Dense

Height/Width: 75 feet tall

Zone: 2

Soil Preference: Well-drained soil

Comments: Use as specimen or in windbreak. Dwarf varieties work well in foundation plantings. Black Hills spruce (P. glauca 'densata') is smaller form of white spruce.

SYCAMORE
Platanus sp.

Buttonwood
P. occidentalis

Type: Deciduous

Fall Foliage: Yellow, brown

Shade Density: Medium to dense

Height/Width: 100 feet/80 feet

Zone: 5

Soil Preference: Moist, well-drained soil

Comments: Use as shade tree. Large, glossy green leaves. Round 1-inch seedpods. Attractive bark, peeling with shades of cream. Can be messy. Subject to fungal blight.

London plane tree
P. x acerifolia

Type: Deciduous

Fall Foliage: Yellow, brown

Shade Density: Medium to dense

Height/Width: 100 feet/80 feet

Zone: 5

Soil Preference: Moist, well-drained soil

Comments: Use as shade tree. Soot-tolerant. Resistant to diseases that affect sycamore. Round seed ball.

TULIP TREE
(Yellow poplar)
Liriodendron tulipifera

Type: Deciduous

Fall Foliage: Yellow

Shade Density: Dense

Height/Width: 100 feet/50 feet

Zone: 5

Soil Preference: Moist, well-drained soil

Comments: Insect- and disease-resistant. Use in wet areas. Massive and impressive if given plenty of space. Two-inch greenish yellow, tulip-shape flowers cover tree in spring after leaves unfurl.

WILLOW
Salix sp.

Babylon weeping
S. babylonica

Type: Deciduous

Fall Foliage: Yellow

Shade Density: Medium

Height/Width: 40 feet/40 feet

Zone: 6

Soil Preference: Moist, well-drained soil

Comments: Fast growing. Use as specimen in wet areas. Pendulous branches sweep the ground. Easily storm and insect damaged. Needs frequent pruning.

White
S. alba

Type: Deciduous

Fall Foliage: Yellow

Shade Density: Medium

Height/Width: 75 feet/60 feet

Zone: 2

Soil Preference: Moist, well-drained soil

Comments: Fast growing. More upright than other varieties. Needs frequent pruning.

Zone Map

The key to successful gardening is knowing what plants are best suited for your area and when to plant them. This is true for every type of gardening. Climate maps, such as the one at right, give a good idea of the extremes in temperature by zones. By choosing plants best adapted to the different zones, and by planting them at the right time, you will have many more successes. The zone-number listings in this book tell you the coldest temperature a plant typically can endure.

The climate in your area is a mixture of many different weather patterns; sun, snow, rain, wind, and humidity. To be a good gardener, you should know, on an average, how cold the garden gets in winter, how much rainfall it receives each year, and how hot or dry it becomes in a typical summer. You can obtain this general information from your state agricultural school or your county extension agent. In addition, acquaint yourself with the mini-climates in your own neighborhood, based on such factors as wind protection gained from a nearby hill, or humidity and cooling offered by a local lake or river. Then carry the research further by studying the microclimates that characterize your own plot of ground.

Here are a few points to keep in mind:

■ Plants react to exposure. Southern and western exposures are sunnier and warmer than northern or eastern ones. Light conditions vary greatly even in a small yard. Match your plants' needs to the correct exposure.

■ Wind can damage many plants, by either drying the soil or knocking over fragile growth. Protect plants from both summer and winter winds to increase their odds of survival and to save yourself the time and energy of staking plants and watering more frequently.

■ Consider elevation, too, when selecting plants. Cold air sweeps down hills and rests in low areas. These frost pockets are fine for some plantings, deadly for others. Plant vegetation that prefers a warmer environment on the tops or sides of hills, never at the bottom.

■ Use fences, the sides of buildings, shrubs, and trees to your advantage. Watch the play of shadows, the sweep of winds, and the flow of snowdrifts in winter. These varying situations are ideal for some plants, harmful to others. In short, always look for ways to make the most of everything your yard has to offer.

THE USDA PLANT HARDINESS MAP
OF THE UNITED STATES AND CANADA

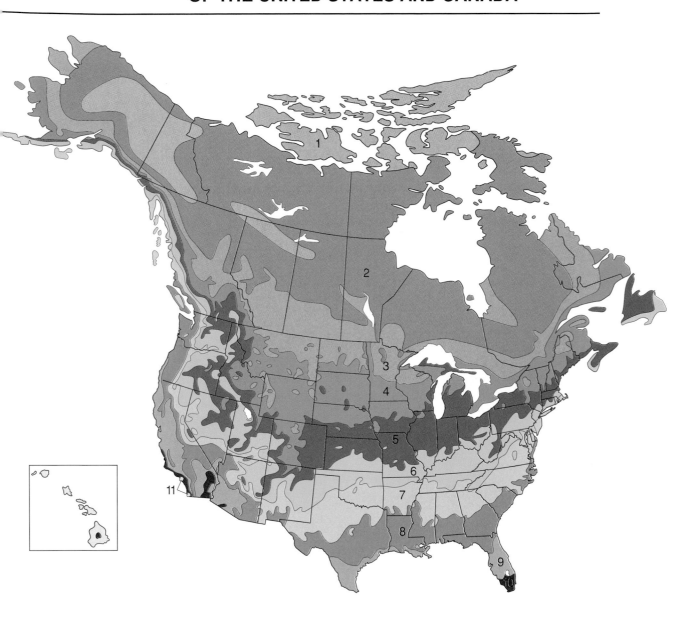

RANGE OF AVERAGE ANNUAL MINIMUM
TEMPERATURES FOR EACH ZONE

	ZONE 1	BELOW -50° F
	ZONE 2	-50° TO -40°
	ZONE 3	-40° TO -30°
	ZONE 4	-30° TO -20°
	ZONE 5	-20° TO -10°
	ZONE 6	-10° TO 0°
	ZONE 7	0° TO 10°
	ZONE 8	10° TO 20°
	ZONE 9	20° TO 30°
	ZONE 10	30° TO 40°
	ZONE 11	ABOVE 40°

Index

A–C

Alder, 42
American beech, 44
American elm, 46
American linden, 52
Amur maple, 53
Atlas cedar, 45
Arborvitae, 42
Ash, 43
Aspen, upright European, 43
Austrian pine, 57
Babylon weeping willow, 61
Balled-and-burlapped trees, 22
Beech, 44
Birch, 44
Box elder, 45
Buckeye, Ohio, 45
Buttonwood sycamore, 60
Canoe birch, 44
Catalpa, 45
Cedar, 45
Chinese elm, 47
Chinese juniper, 51
Choosing a tree, 6
City trees, 19
Colorado spruce, 60
Colors, autumn, 14
Columnar trees, 10, 18
Common horse chestnut, 51
Crab apple, 46
Cucumber tree magnolia, 52
Cutting limbs, 31, 34

D–H

Dense shade trees, 16
Dogwood, 46
Douglas fir, 47
Downy hawthorn, 49
Eastern red cedar juniper, 51
Elm, 46
European alder, 42
European beech, 44
European larch, 52
European linden, small-leaved, 52
European mountain ash, 55
Fall color, trees for, 14, 16
Fast-growing, temporary trees, 16
Feeding, 27
Fertilizer. See feeding
Filtered shade trees, 16
Fir, douglas, 47
Fir, white, 48
Flowering
    dogwood, 46
    trees, 12, 16
Foliage, fall. See specific trees
Fragrant trees, 17
Fruiting trees, 17
Ginkgo, 48
Golden chain, 48

Green ash, 43
Growth rate of trees, 8
Gum, sweet, 49
Hackberry, 49
Hawthorn, 49
Height. See specific trees
Hemlock, 50
Hickory, 50
Honey locust, thornless, 50
Horizontal branched trees, 18
Horse chestnut, 51

I–R

Italian alder, 42
Japanese dogwood, 46
Japanese maple, 54
Juniper, 51
Korean mountain ash, 55
Larch, European, 52
Linden, 52
Lombardy poplar, 52
London plane tree sycamore, 61
Lot size and trees, 8
Magnolia, 52
Maple, 53
Moving trees, 38
Mountain ash, 55
Nonspreading trees, placing, 11
Norway maple, 54
Oak, 55
Ohio buckeye, 45
Older trees, repairing, 36
Olive, Russian, 60
Oriental arborvitae, 42
Painting wounds, 35
Paper birch, 44
Paul's scarlet hawthorn, 49
Pear, 'Bradford' Callery, 57
Pin oak, 55
Pine, 57
Placing trees, 11
Planting trees, 22
Ponderosa pine, 58
Poplar, 59
Pruning and repairs, 28
Pyramidal-shaped trees, 10, 18
Red horse chestnut, 51
Red maple, 54
Red oak, 56
Red pine, 58
Redbud, 59
Repairing trees, 28
River birch, 44
Rounded, 10
Russian olive, 60

S–Z

Saucer magnolia, 53
Scarlet oak, 56
Scotch pine, 58

Selecting a tree, 6
Shapes, tree, 18
Shingle oak, 56
Siberian elm, 47
Silver maple, 54
Single seed hawthorn, 50
Size, tree. See specific trees
Small-leaved European linden, 52
Small trees, placing, 11
Smoothleaf elm, 47
Soil, 8
    preference. See specific trees
Special interest trees, 16
Spreading trees, placing, 11
Spring flowering trees, 12
Spruce, 60
Staking, 25
Sugar maple, 55
Summer flowering trees, 12
Sycamore, 60
Temperatures, 8
Training a young tree, 26
Transplants, 29
Trees
    for dense shade, 16
    for filtered shade, 16
    for special interest, 16
    for fall color, 16
    fast-growing, temporary, 16
    for fragrance, 17
    for fruit, 17
    for spring flowering, 16
    for summer flowering, 16
    for winter interest, 16
    messy and easily broken, 19
    with horizontal branches, 18
Tulip tree, 61
Types and shapes, tree, 10, 16
Vase-shaped trees, 10
Watering, 25, 39
Weeping trees, 10, 18
Width. See specific trees
Willow babylon weeping, 61
Willow oak, 57
Willow white, 61
White ash, 43
White cedar arborvitae, 42
White fir, 48
White oak, 57
White pine, 58
White poplar, 59
White spruce, 60
White willow, 61
Winter,
    interest trees, 16
    preparing trees for, 38
Young trees, training, 26
Zone map, 62
Zones. See specific trees